Managing Editor • Art Worthington

Publishers • Lawrence Siegel & Art Worthington

Design, Writing & Research • Peter Hess

Facilitator • Pamela Thomas

.com

(800) 541-3533

...he story of a man who wanted to keep [the]
world safe for democracy... and meet girls.

VANT YOU

R.U.S. ARMY

STRIPES

COLUMBIA PICTURES PRESENTS
AN IVAN REITMAN FILM
BILL MURRAY
IN
STRIPES
HAROLD RAMIS
WARREN OATES
P.J. SOLES
JOHN CANDY
MUSIC BY ELMER BERNSTEIN SCREENPLAY BY LEN BLUM
& DAN GOLDBERG AND HAROLD RAMIS
PRODUCED BY IVAN REITMAN AND DAN GOLDBERG
DIRECTED BY IVAN REITMAN
R RESTRICTED

BILL MURRAY
Stripes

HARRISON FORD
Raiders
of the
Lost Ark

Indiana Jones
the new hero
[fr]om the creators of
[JA]WS and STAR WARS.

RAIDERS
of the LOST ARK

PARAMOUNT PICTURES Presents A LUCASFILM LTD Production
A STEVEN SPIELBERG Film
Starring HARRISON FORD
KAREN ALLEN · PAUL FREEMAN · RONALD LACEY

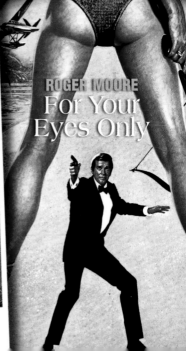

ROGER MOORE
For Your
Eyes Only

It's a hot summer.
Ned Racine is waiting for
something special to happen.

And when it does...
He won't be ready
for the consequences.

BODY
HEAT

As the temperature rises,
the suspense begins.

HALLOWEEN II

ALL NEW

FROM The People Who Brought You "HALLOWEEN"...
More Of The Night He Came Home.

REDS

WARREN BEATTY
DIANE KEATON

On
Golden
Pond

when life is at its finest... when love is at its fullest...

LORD GRADE Presents An ITC Films TPC Films Production A MARK RYDELL Film
KATHARINE HEPBURN HENRY FONDA

TOP BOX OFFICE STARS OF 1981

Clint Eastwood
Sally Field
Harrison Ford
Mel Gibson
Dustin Hoffman
Jessica Lange
Roger Moore
Jack Nicholson
Burt Reynolds
Meryl Streep

Jessica Lange

NEW STARS OF 1981

Albert Brooks
Rae Dawn Chong
Tom Cruise
Jamie Lee Curtis
Rutger Hauer
William Hurt
Steve Martin
Sam Neill
Wallace Shawn
Kathleen Turner

Kathleen Turner

FilmClips

Almost all of **Louis Malle's My Dinner with Andre** portrays a conversation in a tony New York City restaurant between two friends with opposing viewpoints on the nature of reality and the meaning of life.

Dinner's Wallace Shawn (l) & Andre Gregory

Steven Spielberg's **Raiders of the Lost Ark** is the top grossing film of the year and remains one of the biggest money-making movies ever produced.

Candice Bergen (l) & Jacqueline Bisset in Rich and Famous

Rich and Famous is the final film by storied Hollywood director George Cukor, who helmed **Dinner at Eight**, **The Philadelphia Story** and **My Fair Lady**, among many other movie classics.

The fallout continues over **Heaven's Gate**, the 1980 box office bomb that cost United Artists $40 million in unrecovered losses. As a result, the ailing studio is acquired by Metro-Goldwyn-Mayer.

The only thing greater than their pa~~ was their passion for each~~

Michael Cimino's **Heaven's Gate**

Oscars® Presented in 1981
for 1980 films

BEST PICTURE
Ordinary People

BEST ACTOR
Robert De Niro, *Raging Bull*

BEST ACTRESS
Sissy Spacek, *Coal Miner's Daughter*

BEST DIRECTOR
Robert Redford, *Ordinary People*

BEST SUPPORTING ACTOR
Timothy Hutton, *Ordinary People*

BEST SUPPORTING ACTRESS
Mary Steenburgen, *Melvin and Howard*

Oscars® Presented in 1982
for 1981 films

BEST PICTURE
Chariots of Fire

BEST ACTOR
Henry Fonda, *On Golden Pond*

BEST ACTRESS
Katharine Hepburn, *On Golden Pond*

BEST DIRECTOR
Warren Beatty, *Reds*

BEST SUPPORTING ACTOR
John Gielgud, *Arthur*

BEST SUPPORTING ACTRESS
Maureen Stapleton, *Reds*

THE ACADEMY AWARDS

TELEVISION DEBUTS

Dynasty
Entertainment
  Tonight
Falcon Crest
The Fall Guy
Gimme a Break
The Greatest
  American Hero
Hill Street Blues
SCTV Network 90
Simon & Simon
The Smurfs

MINISERIES

Brideshead Revisited
Family Reunion
A Town Like Alice

TOP SHOWS ON THE TUBE

Dallas
60 Minutes
The Jeffersons
Joanie Loves Chachi
Three's Company
Alice
The Dukes of Hazzard
Too Close for Comfort
ABC Monday Night
  Movie
  M*A*S*H
  One Day at a Time
ABC Monday Night
  Football

Sherman Hemsley &
Isabel Sanford of
The Jeffersons

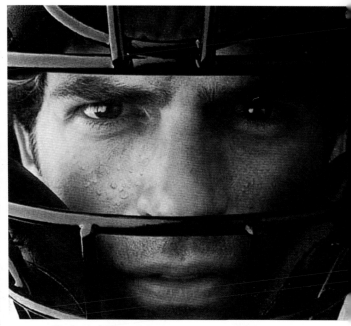

Superb picture and more.
More sharpness. More sound. More channels.

We're moving television into the future. With our new PRP (Peak Resolution Picture) circuit. For 25% more picture sharpness than ever before.* With four speakers, separate amplifiers, even an audio control center. For more fidelity. more true-to-life sound.

With built-in cable tuning (no converter needed). For access to more channels. A hundred and five channels. Zenith System 3 For superb picture. Dependability. And more.

*25 more lines of resolution than previous Zenith models. The PRP Circuit is available on 19" and 25" diagonal System 3 models.

Features available on selected System 3 models and screen sizes. Shown: The Andante, model SM2570E Mediterranean styled console. Genuine Oak wood veneer top and sides with compatible top. Oberne front and base of simulated wood in matching finish. Simulated TV picture.

ZENITH
SYSTEM 3
The quality goes in before the name goes on®

THE **EMMY** AWARDS

SHOWS

COMEDY	*Taxi*
DRAMA	*Hill Street Blues*
VARIETY (SPECIAL)	*Lily: Sold Out*

PERFORMERS

ACTOR (COMEDY)	**Judd Hirsch** *Taxi*
ACTRESS (COMEDY)	**Isabel Sanford** *The Jeffersons*
ACTOR (DRAMA)	**Daniel J. Travanti** *Hill Street Blues*
ACTRESS (DRAMA)	**Barbara Babcock** *Hill Street Blues*

Lily Tomlin (Lily: Sold Out)

Daniel J. Travanti

Pat Sajak replaces **Chuck Woolery** as the host of *Wheel of Fortune.*

●

Comic **Andy Kaufman** appears on the show *Fridays,* where he starts a brawl and pledges his devotion to Jesus.

●

CBS News anchorman **Walter Cronkite** retires after 19 years. **Dan Rather** fills his slot.

Cronkite

The **music video age** dawns when **MTV** debuts on August 1, 1981. A NASA rocket launch and moon landing are the first images broadcast, while an announcer intones *"Ladies and gentlemen, rock 'n' roll."* The first 10 music videos to air on **MTV** are:

1. *Video Killed the Radio Star* **The Buggles**
2. *You Better Run* **Pat Benatar**
3. *She Won't Dance with Me* **Rod Stewart**
4. *You Better You Bet* **The Who**
5. *Little Suzi's on the Up* **Ph.D.**
6. *We Don't Talk Anymore* **Cliff Richard**
7. *Brass in Pocket* **The Pretenders**
8. *Time Heals* **Todd Rundgren**
9. *Take It on the Run* **REO Speedwagon**
10. *Rockin' the Paradise* **Styx**

TOP HITS *in* 1981
Popular Music

Arthur's Theme (Best That You Can Do) Christopher Cross

Endless Love Diana Ross & Lionel Richie

Kiss on My List Daryl Hall & John Oates

(Just Like) Starting Over John Lennon

Bette Davis Eyes Kim Carnes

Jessie's Girl Rick Springfield

Celebration Kool & the Gang

Physical Olivia Newton-John

Rapture Blondie

9 to 5 Dolly Parton

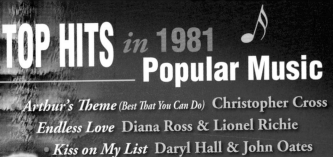

Debbie
Harry
(Blondie)

Diana
Ross

Dolly
Parton

John
Lennon

The new advanced-design GS 1 FM digital keyboard.

ITS ONLY SIMILARITY TO OTHER KEYBOARDS IS THAT IT HAS A KEYBOARD.

Combo Products

THE WAY IT WILL BE.

❀ YAMAHA

U.S. TV audiences get their first look at the Irish group **U2** when they perform "I Will Follow" and "Twilight" on **Tom** **Snyder**'s late night **Tomorrow** show. **The Clash** also make an appearance on Snyder's show, playing "Radio Clash."

Tom Snyder

U2's Bono

The Clash

Paul Simon and Art Garfunkel reunite after a decade to perform before a half million New York fans in a free Central Park concert.

Several new rock bands gain notice by expanding the horizons of Heavy Metal. **Metallica**, **Slayer** and **Anthrax** are exponents of aggressive "Thrash Metal" while **Mötley Crüe** represents glam "Hair Metal."

Metallica

NEW BANDS

**The Bangles
Culture
Club
Depeche
Mode
Dream
Syndicate
Pet Shop
Boys
Sonic
Youth
Tears for
Fears
Wham!**

Early recordings by **the Carter Family, Bob Wills, Roy Acuff, Ernest Tubb, Hank Williams, Johnny Cash, Kitty Wells, Loretta Lynn, Merle Haggard, Willie Nelson** and **George Jones** are among the essential songs included in the 8-volume, denim-clad *Smithsonian Collection of Classic Country Music.*

Bob Wills

Prince (l) & Morris Day

Prince launches a side project called **The Time**. Singer **Morris Day** fronts the funk ensemble while Prince provides instrumental and vocal backing, in addition to writing the material.

Following a stint with **Art Blakey**'s Jazz Messengers and a tour with the **Herbie Hancock** Quartet, young jazz trumpet virtuoso **Wynton Marsalis** records his first solo LP.

Classical Music

Seiji Ozawa conducts the Boston Symphony Orchestra for a recording of *Concerto for Orchestra* by **Roger Sessions**. Sessions will receive the Pulitzer Prize for Music the following year. Ozawa also conducts **Alban Berg**'s *Violin Concerto*, which features the very busy violinist **Itzhak Perlman**. Perlman is awarded a pair of Grammys in 1981, including for Best Classical Performance.

The Best Classical Album of the Year Grammy is awarded to **Sir Georg Solti** for his baton work on **Mahler**'s *Symphony No. 2 in C Minor*.

Itzhak Perlman

MAHLER 2

LONDON

CHICAGO SYMPHONY SOLTI

Minimalist composer **Steve Reich** pays homage to his Jewish heritage with *Tehillim*, a rhythmic piece in four parts which takes the Psalms as its inspiration. It is scored for four women's voices and tuned tambourines without jingles, among other instruments.

Reich

America's most popular sports car.

Sleek. Surefooted. Aerodynamic. That's Mustang. A thoroughbred with the high gas mileage you might not expect from a high-spirited car.

23 EPA EST MPG* · **34** EPA EST HWY*

Choose from a wide range of standard features like rack and pinion steering and modified MacPherson front suspension to an impressive list of options—Michelin TRX radial tires, forged aluminum wheels...even a T-Roof to the sky.

Ford Mustang. Experience why it's America's most popular sports car.

*Estimates for comparison. Your mileage may differ depending on speed, distance and weather. Highway mileage and Calif. estimates lower.

MMMMUSTANG

FORD MUSTANG
FORD DIVISION Ford

on BROADWAY

A Joseph Papp Broadway revival of Gilbert and Sullivan's *The Pirates of Penzance* stars Linda Ronstadt and Kevin Kline.

Linda Ronstadt

London's West End sees the premiere of Andrew Lloyd Webber's musical *Cats*, based on T. S. Eliot's *Old Possum's Book of Practical Cats*.

The history of Motown Records inspires the new musical *Dreamgirls* at New York's Imperial Theatre.

Elaine Paige in Cats

DREAMGIRLS

1981 TONY AWARDS

PLAY
Amadeus
Peter Shaffer (playwright)

MUSICAL
42nd Street
Al Dubin (lyrics)
Harry Warren (music)

ACTOR (PLAY)
Ian McKellen
Amadeus

ACTRESS (PLAY)
Jane Lapotaire
Piaf

DIRECTOR (PLAY)
Peter Hall
Amadeus

ACTOR (MUSICAL)
Kevin Kline
The Pirates of Penzance

ACTRESS (MUSICAL)
Lauren Bacall
Woman of the Year

DIRECTOR (MUSICAL)
Wilford Leach
The Pirates of Penzance

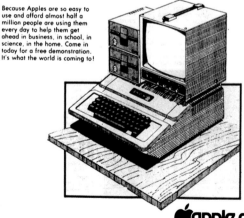

in the **ART** *world*

New York's Museum of Modern Art eyes Hollywood with a pair of exhibitions. *The Hollywood Portrait Photographers 1921–1941* features glamorous pictures of stars by George Hurrell, Cecil Beaton and others. *Ray Harryhausen: Special Effects* salutes the pioneering master of horror movie model-making.

Graffiti gains art world currency with spray paint Picassos **Crash**, **Lee** and **Daze** among those exhibiting at art outposts like Fashion Moda in the South Bronx.

Sculptor **Richard Serra** installs *Tilted Arc*, a 120-foot-long, 12-foot-high rusted steel slab in New York City's Federal Plaza. The government-commissioned art proves unpopular with office workers who call the piece an obstruction and an eyesore. It will be removed eight years later.

1981 Notable Books

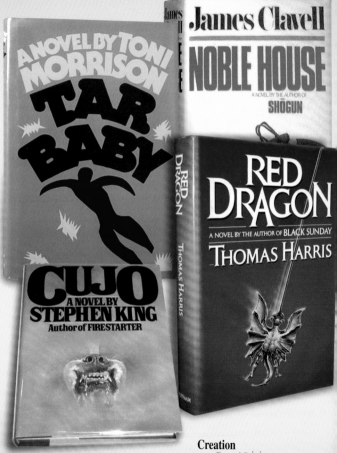

Arabian Nights and Days
Naguib Mahfouz

Creation
Gore Vidal

The Glitter Dome
Joseph Wambaugh

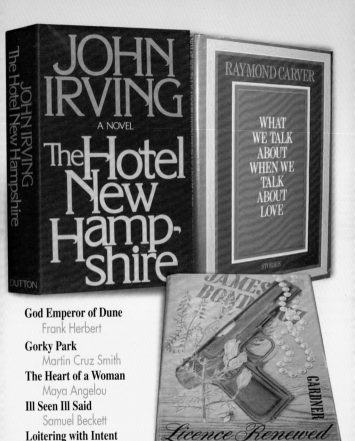

God Emperor of Dune
Frank Herbert

Gorky Park
Martin Cruz Smith

The Heart of a Woman
Maya Angelou

Ill Seen Ill Said
Samuel Beckett

Loitering with Intent
Muriel Spark

The Mismeasure of Man
Stephen Jay Gould

The Mosquito Coast
Paul Theroux

Other People
Martin Amis

A Savage Place
Robert B. Parker

The Third Deadly Sin
Lawrence Sanders

"It's richer. Much richer!"

If you liked the good taste of Sanka*
Decaffeinated Instant or Regular Coffee
yesterday, you'll love the new rich taste
of Sanka today. And if you've only been
thinking of trying Sanka, today's your
day, too. The new taste of Sanka: so
rich it's our best taste ever–to let
you really enjoy being your best.

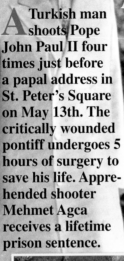

POPE
Survives Assassination Attempt

A Turkish man shoots Pope John Paul II four times just before a papal address in St. Peter's Square on May 13th. The critically wounded pontiff undergoes 5 hours of surgery to save his life. Apprehended shooter Mehmet Agca receives a lifetime prison sentence.

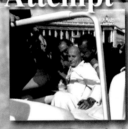

A marble tablet marks the site of the assassination attempt today.

XIII V MCMLXXXI

Reagan: The

| JANUARY 20th | MARCH 30th | JULY 7th |

Ronald Wilson Reagan is sworn in as the 40th U.S. President, succeeding **Jimmy Carter**. Twenty minutes later, 52 Americans held hostage by Iran for 444 days are released.

Reagan is shot in the chest in front of a Washington, DC hotel. **John Hinckley Jr.** also wounds three others in his failed assassination attempt.

Reagan nominates the first woman to the U.S. Supreme Court. **Sandra Day O'Connor** is confirmed by the Senate on September 21st.

Ronald & Nancy Reagan

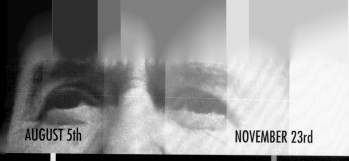

AUGUST 5th

NOVEMBER 23rd

Reagan fires 11,359 striking federal air traffic controllers after they disregard his order to go back to work.

Reagan signs a top secret directive authorizing the Central Intelligence Agency (CIA) to recruit and support Contra rebels in Nicaragua, initiating what will come to be known as the Iran-Contra scandal. It comes to light in 1986 that his authorization enabled the sale of weapons to Iran in order to facilitate the release of U.S. hostages and to raise money for funding the counterinsurgency bent on overthrowing the Nicaraguan government.

Reagan on strikers: "They are in violation of the law and if they do not report for work within 48 hours they have forfeited their jobs and will be terminated."

1981 Advertisement

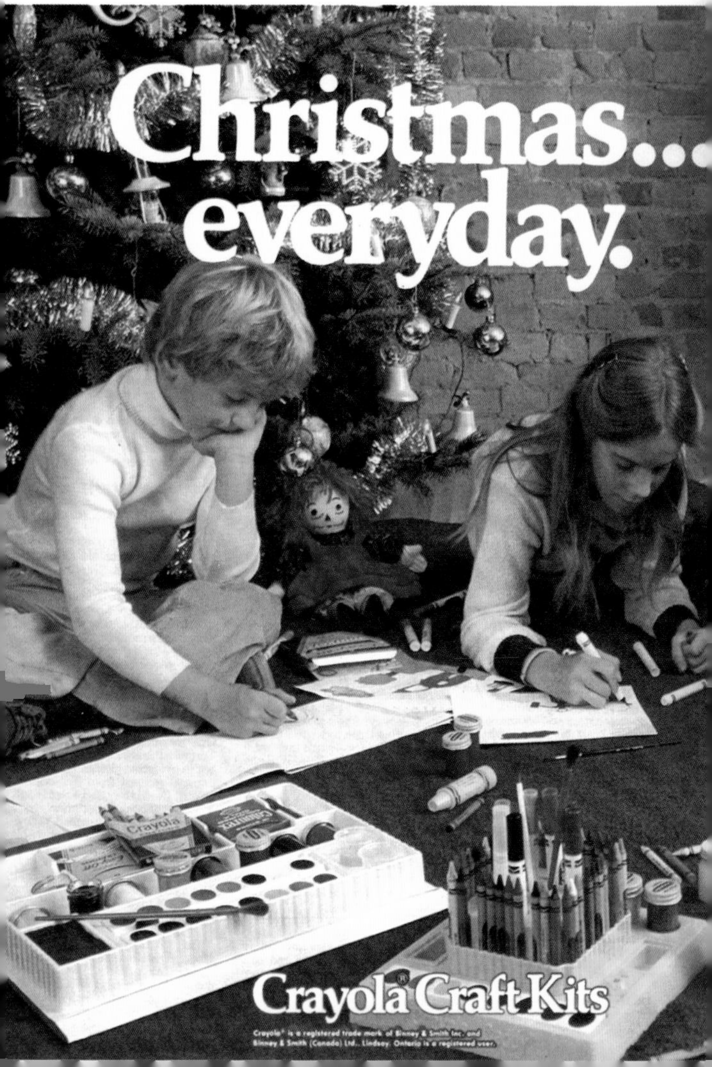

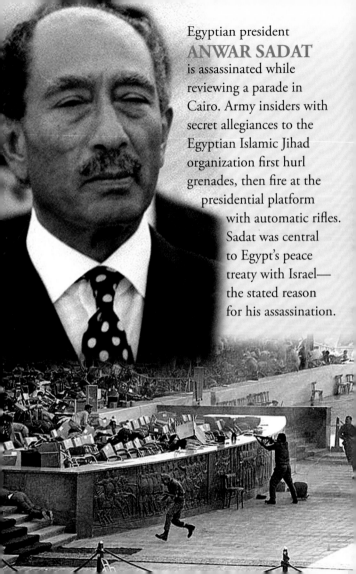

Egyptian president **ANWAR SADAT** is assassinated while reviewing a parade in Cairo. Army insiders with secret allegiances to the Egyptian Islamic Jihad organization first hurl grenades, then fire at the presidential platform with automatic rifles. Sadat was central to Egypt's peace treaty with Israel—the stated reason for his assassination.

England is rocked by violent race riots in Brixton, London and Toxteth, Liverpool. Unemployment and tensions between citizens and police are cited as causes.

Ten Irish republican prisoners perish while on a hunger strike in Maze Prison, Northern Ireland.

SANDS
05 MAY 81

HUGHES
13 MAY 81

McCREESH
21 MAY 81

SON
LY 81

LYNCH
01 AUG 81

DOHERTY
02 AUG 81

O'HARA
21 MAY 81

McDONNELL
08 JULY 81

Jiang Qing, wife of the late Mao Zedong, is tried for "heinous" crimes of persecution which she ordered during China's Cultural Revolution. She is found guilty and sentenced to death.

Libyan dictator Muammar al-Gaddafi sends 2 jets to intercept 2 U.S. fighters over the Gulf of Sidra. Libya's jets are destroyed.

300 civilians are killed and swaths of buildings are destroyed when Israel bombs Beirut while targeting militant Palestinian groups. Israel is condemned worldwide for its action.

Fearful of strides made by the Solidarity freedom movement, prime minister General Wojciech Jaruzelski imposes martial law in Poland.

Solidarność

1981 Advertisement

BLACK MAGIC

There are many compelling reasons to own a Capri from
Lincoln-Mercury. For example, you can choose from
a selection of options to satisfy the most
sophisticated demands.
• Turbo-charged engine • Moonroof
• TRX tires, wheels and suspension
• New 5-speed transmission

• Leather seat cushion inserts • Premium sound system
• AM/FM stereo cassette. But the most compelling
reason for you to own a Capri is no reason
that can be put into words. Call it a touch of
sexiness. Or a touch of mystery. Or perhaps
a touch of magic.
LINCOLN-MERCURY DIVISION *Ford*

CAPRI FROM LINCOLN-MERCURY

The standard engine/drive train combination is rated 25 EPA EST., 38 HWY EST. Compare to estimated MPG of other cars. Your mileage may differ depending on speed, weather and trip length. Actual highway MPG and California estimate less.

QUICKSILVER

With our new metallic
paint treatment, you
may be attracted
to the 1981 Capri on
the basis of its looks
alone. But there are
more compelling
reasons to own one
than what merely
meets the eye.
   Choose such
sophisticated
options as • The
5-speed manual
transmission • TRX
tires, wheels and
suspension • The
new T-roof • Four-
speaker premium
sound system

• Reclining Recaro
seats • Leather-
wrapped steering
wheel.
And with the
standard engine
and drive train, the
1981 Capri is rated at
25 EPA EST. MPG,
34 EST. HWY.
But the most
compelling reason
to own a Capri is
no reason that can
be put into words.
Call it a touch of
sexiness. Or a
touch of mystery.
Or perhaps a touch
of magic.

CAPRI
LINCOLN-MERCURY DIVISION *Ford*

CAPRI FROM LINCOLN-MERCURY

*Compare to estimated MPG of other cars. Your mileage may differ depending on speed, weather conditions, and trip length.   Actual highway mileage and California ratings lower. Buy or Lease at your Lincoln-Mercury dealer.

29th July 1981

A worldwide television audience estimated at 700 million tunes in to see the wedding of Charles, the Prince of Wales, and Lady Diana Spencer at London's St. Paul's Cathedral on July 29th.

21-year-old undergraduate **Maya Lin**'s spare, elegant design for the Vietnam Veterans Memorial is unanimously selected by a jury of architects and sculptors over 1,420 competing submissions.

The first recognized cases of AIDS are reported in 5 Los Angeles homosexual men.

Capital punishment is abolished in France.

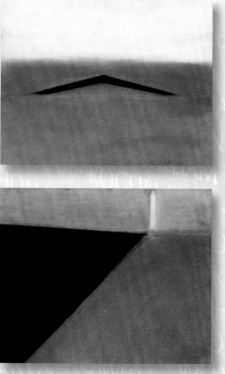

Maya Lin's original submitted drawings.

Tampomas

Disasters

January 6 – Double-decker boat Novo Amapo capsizes on the Amazon River, Macapa, Brazil; 230 dead • •

January 23 – 6.8 magnitude earthquake in Sichuan, China; 150 dead • • **January 27** – Indonesian passenger ship Tampomas II burns and capsizes in the Java Sea; 580 dead • •

February 8 – Stampede at Karaiskaki Stadium, Athens; 21 dead, 54 injured • • **February 10** – Fire at the Las Vegas Hilton hotel-casino; 8 dead, 198 injured • •

February 14 – Fire at Stardust nightclub in Dublin, Ireland; 48 dead, 214 injured • • **June 6** – Seven coaches of passenger train fall off tracks into the River Kosi in Bihar, India; approx. 800 dead • • **July 17** – Skywalk collapses in the Hyatt Regency atrium, Kansas City, MO; 114 dead • • **October 16** – Explosions in a coal mine at Hokkaidō, Japan; 93 dead.

Bihar

HILTON BURN

Hotel Fire Kills 8;
Hundreds Injured

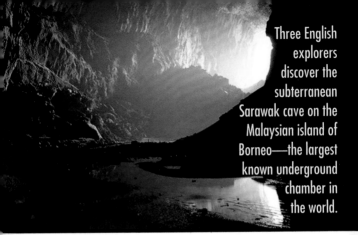

Three English explorers discover the subterranean Sarawak cave on the Malaysian island of Borneo—the largest known underground chamber in the world.

There she is...
Miss America for *1981* is **Susan Powell** *from Elk City, Oklahoma, far left,* and *Miss Universe* is **Irene Sáez** *representing Venezuela*

THE YORKSHIRE RIPPER

Police in Sheffield, England arrest 34-year-old truck driver **Peter Sutcliffe**, whom they suspect of being the infamous Yorkshire Ripper. Sutcliffe's brutal serial killing spree began in 1975. He typically bludgeoned, tied and knifed young women, some of them prostitutes. Police record his calm descriptions of his crimes— 13 murders and 7 attempted murders in all—for which he is sentenced to life in prison.

Corrections officer **DONNA PAYANT** is slain by **Lemuel Smith**, who is serving a 50-year sentence for two murders in New York's Greenhaven Correctional Facility. Payant is the first female on-duty prison guard ever killed in the U.S.

WONDERLAND MURDERS

Four people are found brutally murdered in a house on Wonderland Avenue in L.A.'s Laurel Canyon. The victims had conspired with porn star **John Holmes** to rob the home of drug dealer **Eddie Nash**, who savagely beats Holmes until he leads him to the robbers, where Nash takes his retribution.

Holmes

THE ATLANTA CHILD MURDERS

23-year-old aspiring music producer **Wayne Williams** is arrested as a key suspect in the disappearances and strangulation murders of approximately 2 dozen African American children in Atlanta over a 2-year span. Though Williams is spotted near a crime scene, he vehemently denies the charges, even after failing a polygraph exam. Williams is sentenced to two life terms in 1982, but the case remains controversial because his conviction is only for two unrelated adult murders and no evidence has been uncovered to date conclusively connecting him to the slain children.

The remains of 6-year-old ADAM JOHN WALSH are discovered 2 weeks after his abduction from a Florida Sears store. His murder gains national notoriety and Adam's father, **John Walsh**, becomes an advocate for victims of violent crime, gaining renown as the host of the television show AMERICA'S MOST WANTED.

Machine gun-wielding MORRIS EDWIN ROBERT enters the FBI section of the Atlanta, Georgia Federal Building, where he seizes hostages. Following a 3-hour standoff, the hostages are rescued and Robert is killed by federal agents.

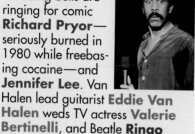

Wedding bells are ringing for comic **Richard Pryor**—seriously burned in 1980 while freebasing cocaine—and **Jennifer Lee**. Van Halen lead guitarist **Eddie Van Halen** weds TV actress **Valerie Bertinelli**, and Beatle **Ringo Starr** and actress **Barbara Bach** tie the knot. And the fictional nuptials of *General Hospital* soap characters **Luke** and **Laura** are second only to the Charles and Diana wedding in TV viewership.

Elizabeth Taylor makes her Broadway debut in *The Little Foxes*. When her part in the stage drama makes news, almost $1 million in tickets are sold in the first week.

Natalie Wood drowns after apparently slipping and falling overboard while on her yacht, anchored off Southern California's Catalina Island. The 43-year-old veteran actress had spent an evening of heavy onboard drinking with current co-star **Christopher Walken** and her husband, **Robert Wagner**.

Wood

Reggae superstar **Bob Marley** succumbs at age 36 to malignant melanoma, first diagnosed in 1977.

Folk rock singer/songwriter **Harry Chapin** dies after an automobile accident in New York, aged 38.

Marley

Rita Jenrette, the wife of disgraced and convicted "Abscam" congressman John Jenrette, bares all for *Playboy* magazine, as do actresses **Barbara Bach**, **Maud Adams** and (for the 3rd time) **Bo Derek**.

Rita Jenrette

AEROSMITH lead singer **Steven Tyler**'s injuries from a motorcycle crash leave him hospitalized and unable to record or tour for months.

John Phillips of THE MAMAS AND THE PAPAS pleads guilty to drug possession charges, reducing a long jail term to 30 days plus community service.

Eric Clapton suffers injuries in a Seattle car crash days after being released from the hospital for ulcer treatment. The rock guitarist admits to an alcohol problem.

Eric Clapton

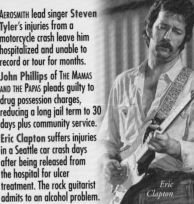

People *Weekly* fills us in on their selection of the Most Intriguing People of 1981. Among those making the cut of 25: the **Ronald Reagans**, **Mick Jagger**, **Princess Diana**, **Lena Horne**, **Tom Selleck**, **Ted Turner**, new Supreme Court justice **Sandra Day O'Connor**, **Harrison Ford**, **Barbara Mandrell** and tennis ace **John McEnroe**.

And, **People** prints a reader's poll giving a thumbs-up to **Alan Alda** and **Victoria Principal** (favorite male and female TV stars), **Bo Derek** and **Robert Redford** (the best-looking stars) and **Dan Rather** (favorite TV news anchor). The news is not so good, however, for **Suzanne Somers** and **Carroll O'Connor**, who are voted the most boring TV stars.

Mick Jagger, Nancy Reagan, Dan Rather, Lena Horne

MAGAZINES

Detective Comics — BATMAN

DOUBLE-FEATURE MOVIE ISSUE! MAD 90c

CINEFANTASTIQUE
ARE THESE THE SCARIEST MEN IN AMERICA?

E.T. · FILMS ILLUS

TiGER beat
FULL COLOR PIN-UPS! 2 GORGEOUS CENTERFOLDS!
MICHAEL or DANNY—Which One Do You Really Love?
DAYTIME GUYS, LEIF, SHAWN, TV'S TOP GIRLS

BURT REYNOLDS: HAS THIS LADIES' MAN RUN OUT OF LADIES?
Modern Screen
JACKIE SMITH & OLIVIA NEWTON-JOHN
CAN ANY MAN EVER MEASURE UP?
Is She Too Perfect For Her Own Good?
Is She Too Cautious To Say 'I Do'?

BONUS: MY SECRET LIFE WITH THE ROLLING STONES
Us
DYNASTY'S DARLING

EGNANT SECRET ROYAL BRIDE
LIC: the cle icine
OSMOND: N'T A BABY
Farrah's after Dr's age-man
Gable's amazing
Flirting can save your marriage

OUi
SUPERSTARS SPEAK OUT

WET

LAYGIRL
ve Interview
VESTER LLONE

KUNG-FU INSIDE
THE ULTIMATE IN MARTIAL ARTS COVERAGE
LEO GAJE:

V-8 VEGA HOW TO
HOT RODDIN
DO-IT YOURSELF

New for '81

Candie's®

TCBY®

GUESS

Q®
Quiznos® Sub

Quark®

BELIZE

ASTRO BLASTER

DONKEY KONG

FROGGER

MS. PAC-MAN

BOEING 767

DELOREAN
DMC-12

TEST
TUBE
BABIES
(U.S.)

THE SPACE
SHUTTLE

IBM 5150
PC

FRANCE'S
TGV
HIGH-SPEED
TRAIN

1981 Advertisement

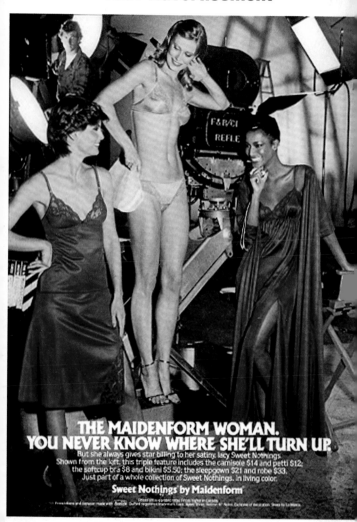

Fashion '81

*Ruffles and floral prints
on sheer overlays mark
the new romantic look.*

*Designer
jeans are
all the rage
and everybodys
got their own spin—
Gloria Vanderbilt,
Guess, Calvin Klein,
even "Her Levi's"
exclusively for gals.*

Pastel flared jeans paired with coordinated T-shirts.

Betsey Johnson long knits over striped leggings with boots.

Madras for tykes.

A collarless jacket and accessories lend casual elegance to scooped tops.

1981 Advertisement

Designer jeans for men extend to lace-up fronts.

Muted colors predominate in menswear, with shortened, flat-bottom neckties.

1981 Advertisement

Phil and Steve Mahre, World Cup Race at Aspen

You have what it takes to win.
Help support the U.S. Ski Team.

The U.S. Ski Team is on a winning streak. They need your help to keep it going.

World Cup victories by Phil Mahre and Tamara McKinney highlighted the 1981 season. The Team's wins provide high hopes for the 1982 World Championships.

Our Alpine and Nordic Teams are not subsidized by the government. These fine athletes devote years of their lives training to win. They depend on you, the American public, to support their efforts. Please send your tax-deductible donations to the U.S. Ski Educational Foundation, Box 100M, Park City, Utah 84060.

Please help.

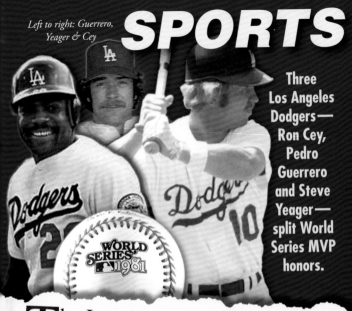

Left to right: Guerrero, Yeager & Cey

SPORTS

Three Los Angeles Dodgers — Ron Cey, Pedro Guerrero and Steve Yeager — split World Series MVP honors.

The Los Angeles Dodgers beat the New York Yankees 4 games to 2 to win the World Series in a strike-shortened season.

Most Valuable Player

National League
Mike Schmidt (Philadelphia)

American League
Rollie Fingers (Milwaukee)

Cy Young Award

National League
Fernando Valenzuela (L.A.)

American League
Rollie Fingers (Milwaukee)

Rookie of the Year

National League
Fernando Valenzuela (L.A.)

American League
Dave Righetti (N.Y.)

Home Run Leaders

National League
Mike Schmidt
(Philadelphia, 31)

American League
Bobby Grich (California, 22)
Eddie Murray (Baltimore, 22)

Mike Schmidt

FOOTBALL

SUPERBOWL XVI
San Francisco 49ers over
Cincinnati Bengals, 26-21

67th ROSE BOWL
Michigan Wolverines over
Washington Huskies,
23-6

HEISMAN TROPHY
Marcus Allen,
USC, RB

NCAA COLLEGE
CHAMPIONS
Clemson Tigers

USC FOOTBALL

MARCUS ALLEN
Heisman Trophy
Candidate

BASKETBALL

NBA CHAMPIONS
Boston Celtics over
Houston Rockets, 4-2

MVP:
Cedric Maxwell, Boston

NBA SEASON SCORING
LEADER
Adrian Dantley, Utah
(30.7 avg.)

NCAA CHAMPIONS
Indiana over
North Carolina, 63-50

*Adrian
Dantley*

BOXING

In a match promoted as the "Drama in Bahama," Muhammad Ali loses to Trevor Berbick on December 11th, the last fight of Ali's career.

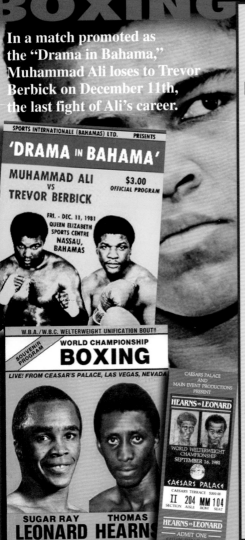

SPORTS INTERNATIONALE (BAHAMAS) LTD.   PRESENTS

'DRAMA IN BAHAMA'

MUHAMMAD ALI
vs
TREVOR BERBICK

$3.00
OFFICIAL PROGRAM

FRI. - DEC. 11, 1981
QUEEN ELIZABETH
SPORTS CENTRE
NASSAU,
BAHAMAS

W.B.A./W.B.C. WELTERWEIGHT UNIFICATION BOUT!!

SOUVENIR PROGRAM

WORLD CHAMPIONSHIP
BOXING

LIVE! FROM CEASAR'S PALACE, LAS VEGAS, NEVADA

SUGAR RAY   THOMAS
LEONARD   HEARNS

CAESARS PALACE
AND
MAIN EVENT PRODUCTIONS
PRESENT

HEARNS vs LEONARD

WORLD WELTERWEIGHT
CHAMPIONSHIP
SEPTEMBER 16, 1981

CAESARS PALACE

CAESARS TERRACE $200.00
II   204   MM   104
SECTION   AISLE   ROW   SEAT

HEARNS vs LEONARD

ADMIT ONE
CAESARS PALACE $200.00
SEPTEMBER 16, 1981

APRIL 11th

Larry Holmes retains his WBC heavyweight title by defeating **Trevor Berbick** in a unanimous decision.

AUGUST 21st

Salvador Sánchez KOs **Wilfredo Gómez** in the 8th to retain the WBC featherweight crown.

SEPTEMBER 16th

Sugar Ray Leonard TKOs **Thomas Hearns** in 14 rounds to unify the world welterweight championships.

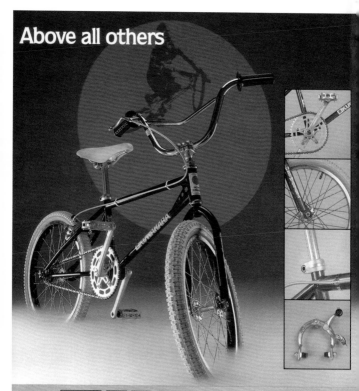

GOLF

MASTERS
Tom Watson

U.S. OPEN
Men: David Graham
Women: Pat Bradley

U.S. AMATEUR
Nathaniel Crosby

BRITISH OPEN
Bill Rogers

PGA CHAMPIONSHIP
Men: Larry Nelson
Women: Donna Caponi

Tom Watson

TENNIS

WIMBLEDON
Men: John McEnroe
Women: Chris Evert

U.S. OPEN TENNIS
SINGLES CHAMPS
Men: John McEnroe
Women: Tracy Austin

FRENCH OPEN
Men: Björn Borg
Women: Hana Mandlíková

Chris Evert

John McEnroe

1981 Advertisement

What it is is beautiful.

Have you ever seen anything like it? Not just what she's made, but how proud it's made her. It's a look you'll see whenever children build something all by themselves. No matter what they've created.

Younger children build for fun. LEGO®Universal Building Sets for children ages 3 to 7 have colorful bricks, wheels, and friendly LEGO people for lots and lots of fun.

Older children build for realism. LEGO Universal Building Sets for children 7–12 have more detailed pieces, like gears, rotors, and treaded tires for more realistic building. One set even has a motor.

LEGO Universal Building Sets will help your children discover something very, very special: themselves.

LEGO® is a registered trademark of Interlego A.G.
© 1981 LEGO Group

Universal Building Sets

744 Ages 7-12

7-12 years old

3-7 years old

LEGO

Born in 1981

Josh Groban

Alicia Keys

Justin Timberlake

Serena Williams

Elijah Wood

Jessica Alba	Beyoncé Knowles
Amanda Beard	Adriana Lima
Rachel Bilson	Eli Manning
Gretchen Bleiler	Sienna Miller
Barbara P. Bush	Natalie Portman
Jenna Bush	Nicole Richie
Hayden Christensen	Kelly Rowland
Roger Federer	Jamie-Lynn Sigler
Josh Groban	Britney Spears
Paris Hilton	Julia Stiles
Jennifer Hudson	Justin Timberlake
Alicia Keys	Ivanka Trump
Anna Kournikova	Serena Williams
Joseph Gordon-Levitt	Elijah Wood

DIED IN 1981

Joe Louis

Nelson Algren
novelist

Omar N. Bradley
5-star U.S. general

Hoagy Carmichael
songwriter

René Clair
film director

Moshe Dayan
Israeli general

Melvyn Douglas
actor

Gloria Grahame
actress

Bill Haley
musician

Edith Head
costume designer

William Holden
actor

Lotte Lenya
singer/actress

Joe Louis
boxer

William Saroyan
writer

Mary Lou Williams
jazz pianist

William Wyler
film director